NO FEELING LASTS FOREVER

noticing emotions in ourselves and others

SARA OLSHER

Hi! My name is Mia.

And this is Stuart.
He says he is one hundred and twelve years old
(and thirteen days).

Every day, I have **LOTS** of emotions.
We all do!

HAPPY!

sleepy

Wake up, Stuart...

GRUMPY

Emotions happen all day long.

They aren't good or bad.

Some emotions have a lot of energy, like anger or excitement.
Your body wants to jump or run or yell or kick!

CREATIVE

bored...
sooo
bored...

Excited!

IMPATIENT

Other emotions have low energy, like sadness or loneliness.
Those feelings might make us want to lay down or sleep.

HAPPY!

Excited!

Some emotions **FEEL** better than others.

It's normal to want some feelings, like sadness or anger, to go away.

But no one feels happy all the time, and no feeling lasts forever!

Emotions happen for a lot of reasons.

Sometimes we have emotions because of
what's happening around us.

Lots of noise can make some people feel *ANXIOUS*.

People laughing and joking can make us feel

Sometimes we have emotions because we **NEED** something.

Maybe we are hungry and need a snack.
Maybe we are tired and need to rest.
Maybe we are lonely and need a hug.

Let's ask your body what it needs!

Sometimes all you need to feel better

is a hug,

or a deep breath,

or a snack.

Sad

JOYFUL

HUNGRY

HAPPY!

SCARED

SHY

PROUD

so many feelings every day!

Calm

Sad

When we learn to use **WORDS** to talk about emotions,

having big feelings is less frustrating, because we can say what happened and ask for what we need.

And when we can understand how **OTHER** people are feeling, we know if they are in the mood to play a game or be silly...

... or if maybe being silly would make them feel bad, because right now they need a hug or some extra kindness.

Sometimes you can tell
what someone is feeling
by looking at their face.

What do you think I am feeling?

ANGRY   **SHY**   **DISAPPOINTED**

CONFUSED   **DEPRESSED**   **FRUSTRATED**

READY

BORED

SAD

NERVOUS

CREATIVE

SCARED

EXCITED

HAPPY

RELAXED

PROUD

We can find clues in their eyes, their eyebrows, their mouths ... even their hands!

Sometimes big emotions can scare us.
We worry that the emotion in our body will
get too big or strong, or it will never end.

But **NO FEELING LASTS FOREVER**
... even the really big ones.

When we have **BIG** feelings and **BIG** emotions, getting that energy *out* by

crying

or running

or kicking a ball

can make us feel better.

So can talking about our feelings or getting a hug from a safe person.

A grown-up can handle our big feelings.

 GRUMPY

 WORRIED

CREATIVE

PROUD

READY

When we learn how to talk about our emotions,
we can tell other people what we need.

When we notice other people's emotions,
we can be better friends.

Emotions happen all day long, and none of them last forever.

How do **you** feel?

FURIOUS!

Excited!

IMPATIENT

Calm

SHY

UNCOMFORTABLE

Sad

depressed.

Hi! my name is Sara. Nice to meet you!

I wrote this book (& lots of others!) because I like to draw + help people.

Things I LOVE!

- reading
- Dancing (Badly)
- my family
- nature
- animals
- candy
- Rainbows
- Quiet time

I live in a state known for trees + rain, in a city nicknamed "the cherry city."

I do all my drawings on an iPad with an Apple pencil

I live with my daughter and our two cats, Waffle + Batman.

One day, I want a goat, and I want to name him **CAULIFLOWER!**

Hey Parents!

You don't have to be a superhero to be an *incredible* parent.

There's no shortage of parenting information out there.
But most of us feel like we can barely make it through the day
... let alone thoughtfully develop the skills our kids need.

At Mighty + Bright, we've figured out how to:

- Incorporate emotional + mental wellbeing into your day-to-day life

- Learn a common language with your kids

- Make your parenting life easier

- Reduce meltdowns and underlying anxiety

  ...with no thick parenting books,
  (and no digital parenting courses.)

Find more books like this and tools that'll totally change your family

SCAN THIS USING YOUR PHONE
or visit: mightyandbright.com/emotions

We believe it shouldn't take *more* effort to guide your kids the way you want to guide them.
It just takes a different perspective.

Book Sara for school visits and
public speaking at saraolsher.com

mighty
+
bright

Published by Mighty + Bright
mightyandbright.com

ISBN: 979-8-9867765-2-1

want to tell
Sara something?
Send a letter!

Sara Olsher
13203 SE 172ND Ave
Suite 166, #1121
Happy Valley, Oregon
97086

Made in the USA
Middletown, DE
15 November 2024

64638063R00018